California RCFE Insurance Guide

Getting the Protection You Need in a Changing Environment

Charley Beals, LUTCF, CSS

Disclaimer: This book is written to be a guide. I am only making suggestions of the most common traps that many RCFE owners fall into when selecting insurance. Only you and your Professional Insurance Agent can choose the proper coverages for your business.

California RCFE Insurance Guide

Published by:
90-Minute Books
302 Martinique Drive
Winter Haven, FL 33884
www.90minutebooks.com

Published in the United States of America

ISBN-13: 978-0692604526
ISBN-10: 0692604529

For more information on 90-Minute Books including finding out how you can
publish your own lead generating book, visit www.90minutebooks.com or call
(863) 318-0464

Here's What's Inside…

Charley Beals and his team did a terrific job finding exactly the kind of insurance I needed. He was professional, responsive and went out of his way to ensure the coverage and price were right. I would not hesitate to recommend Charley Beals for your insurance needs.

Brian Wenger
An Everlasting Spring RCFE

Charley and his team have been a godsend at a time when insurance regulation has become so complex and overwhelming. As an owner of several RCFEs, I have more than enough on my plate and don't need additional stress worrying about compliance or feeling unprotected in today's highly litigious environment. Charley provides me tremendous relief and assurance that my business is protected and that I am getting the optimal coverage for my money. He is highly knowledgeable, personable and attentive to my needs. I am fortunate to have him as my agent, advisor and friend.

David A. Flood
Compassionate Care RCFE

I have been in business for over 25 years. I own a General Construction Company and I also own two RCFE Homes in the Thousand Oaks area.

Finding a knowledgeable, trustworthy and ethical insurance agent is tough these days, I feel I found this with Charley Beals.

Charley is dedicated to his business, clients and will go the extra mile for them, even if it's <u>NOT</u> beneficial for him, here is a good example, he looked into my Construction business and advised me to stay with the coverage I currently have, because it was best for me.

I strongly encourage people to give Charley a chance to look into their insurance needs. Charley has taken my numerous coverages from personal to business, and sent them out for bidding with different carriers. He not only saved me thousands of dollars, but has made it easy to manage my insurance needs. I don't guarantee much in business, but I will guarantee this, people or companies that allow Charley to look into their insurance coverages will <u>NOT</u> be disappointed, and if they don't, it would be a <u>BIG</u> mistake.

I would personally like to give my thanks and gratitude to Charley. During my coverage, I had lapsed with one of my payments. I thought the insurance company was withdrawing my monthly payments automatically from my bank account, and they weren't, so they had canceled my coverage, Charley immediately called me and warned me I didn't have coverage on my trucks. Without this, I would have been driving my trucks thinking I had coverage. Once again, <u>THANK YOU</u> Charley for protecting my best interest.

These are just a few testimonies on how I have benefited by Charley's services.

Ruben Carmona
Applegate Homes, Inc.

Charley Beals has established himself as THE expert in the field of insurance for Residential Care Facilities. I have had the pleasure of working with him personally, and on behalf of many clients. His knowledge of the intricacies of the industry is unparalleled, and his ability to get his clients phenomenal coverage at affordable rates amazes even me, and I've been in the industry over a decade.

Justin M. Levi
ElderCare Consulting Group

In short, I am extremely pleased with the professional service that you have provided me over the past year. You have managed to accomplish things that others only talk about. You have also displayed a deep understanding of the needs in our industry. You think out of the box, which has proven to be quite fruitful for us.

Michael Gabai
Ayres Residential Care Homes

I have been very pleased with the attention and detail that Charley has provided in helping our company obtain the proper insurance for our business. Charley helps you to make informed decisions regarding your policy. Charley is very thorough and is a pleasure to work with.

Shelley Zander
At Regency Ranch Residential Care
At Sunny Hills Home Care

There isn't a better use of my time then stating my enthusiasm for Charley Beals of the Beals Insurance Group. He has consistently offered my clients his expertise and his full knowledge, and in such a kind, easy-going manner that my clients find so appealing, especially as they need to trust their insurance guy! My clients depend on Charley's understanding of the insurance choices for RCFE operators and how to incorporate those needs into a nice neat insurance package that won't keep them awake at night. Charley is my only go-to guy for my clients' insurance needs.

Rolanda Reeder Conversino
Consultants on Aging

Charley Beals has distinguished himself above other insurance agents and brokers. I have been a lawyer for over 30 years, and I routinely work with insurance agents and brokers. Without hesitation, I wholeheartedly recommend Charley Beals and the Beals Insurance Group for all insurance needs. Charley has provided the utmost care and professional services to both me and my clients. His continuous willingness to help, answer questions, and ensure that the proper insurance is secured exemplifies his vast knowledge of the insurance industry.

Sincerely,
Garry S. Malin
Law Offices of Garry S. Malin

I am happy to recommend Charley Beals of the Beals Insurance Group. He has a place in his heart for RCFEs (his grandmother lived in one). He has taken the time to learn about the business and he has helped many RCFEs find the right coverage for a fair price. Charley and his staff are dedicated to finding the right policies for your facility.

Richard Chace
Elderlink and California Registry Referral Services

Charley, is the man! As a newcomer to the adult care industry, RCFEs in particular, there was a lot of information that I needed to catch up on, really quick. Talking with Charley, I began to realize very quickly that he is the industry expert. Additionally, he took the time to answer all of my questions and go over all of the minutia that was involved. I have owned many businesses, and own a lot of properties. I have never had an insurance guy walk me through every detail, as Charley has done. I give Charley my highest recommendation and personally cannot wait to own additional facilities so that we can do more business together.

Regards,
David Ebrami
Mishkan Senior Care RCFE

Introduction

When I meet a new client I like to get to know them and their business model. One of my favorite introductory questions is: "How did you get into the business of Residential Care Facilities for the Elderly (RCFE)?" Out of the hundreds of clients I represent all over California, there is a common thread. Owners and administrators always begin by talking about their mother, father, or loved one. Someone they knew well had been diagnosed with either Alzheimer's, dementia, or some other crippling malady, and they couldn't find the type of care they needed or wanted for their loved one. Ultimately what happened was they ended up quitting their job to become a full-time caregiver and found it so rewarding that they wanted to continue doing the work.

I have a very similar story. My grandmother Darlene, who used to take me fishing off the Santa Monica Pier when I was a boy, spent the last six years of her life in a residential care facility. This took a huge toll on our family. After seeing the effect on my family both emotionally and financially, I wanted to give back. Because of my years of experience in Commercial Insurance, I am able to provide a superior service at the absolute best value with an everyone-wins attitude. By prescribing and reviewing the correct coverages for each individual Care Home, I have created an environment that then translates into better care for our loved ones at a time they are most vulnerable. Most caregivers are very good at being caregivers, but they are completely overwhelmed with the fluid nature of the Commercial insurance marketplace in California.

By producing this booklet, I hope to take some of the mystery out of the commercial insurance equation and simplify the process by breaking down and answering the most common causes of loss and what the RCFE owner needs to know to protect their residents and their business.

To Your Success!

Charley Beals

Why Don't More RCFE Owners Have the Right Insurance Protection?

Susan: I'm excited to be here with Charley Beals. Charley is going to share his thoughts and ideas on how to get the proper insurance protection for your RCFE. Welcome Charley!

Charley: Thank you Susan. I'm glad to be here.

Susan: So am I. Let's start off with why don't more RCFE owners have the insurance that they need, Charley?

Charley: I have found that this is truly a 24/7 business with the owners acting as both Chief Administrator and Owner. They must constantly deal with all of the issues of running a small business: such as working with and training employees, making sure payroll is handled properly, taxes, keeping up with and conforming to all the laws and legislation and paying all the bills. The list is endless, and paying the bills is a never ending cycle. They continually market to keep the beds full and preserve cash flow, while maintaining a hopefully profitable business. They do their best to meet the demands of family members. They pull long hours and on top of it all while trying to maintain some type of reasonable personal life. It's exhausting. Then you add the ever changing Federal and State laws regarding Care Homes and Employee regulations …. The entire process can drive them nuts and can make them feel like the business is running them, not that they are running the business. With all they have to juggle on a daily basis, it's no wonder most owners are in desperate need of professional advice when it comes to the field of commercial insurance.

As you may know, the state of California is in a cash crunch right now. They are looking for ways to draw a more money from everybody.

A caregiver must be a compassionate, loving, patient person – someone who takes a moment to sit and chat, hold somebody's hand, fix a blanket, and adjust a pillow. The business owners' role is completely different from that of a caregiver, not just in terms of tasks, but also the opposite personality requirements between the two positions; they really need a business manager and a caregiver manager. However, the cash flow of the business doesn't usually allow the ability to buy the necessary and needed talent.

Since most RCFEs don't have the resources to wear all of those hats, they are forced to outsource their professional needs and manage those people as business partners. It is a delicate balance running a business like this.

Insurance is a complicated business with a language of its own. Two policies can be compared side by side with similar but not equal coverage, showing vastly different costs. Why is that? The language and details of the policy control the cost and (most importantly) the amount of coverage. "You get what you pay for" is especially pertinent to insurance. A simple endorsement, buried in the policy language where it won't be read, could remove a necessary coverage that this particular business needs. That caring person, who started in this business to help people, should not be penalized because they do not speak insurance.

They should be supported and honored for offering a gift to our ailing loved ones. Other than payroll, the cost of insurance is the greatest expense that small businesses will see. If an owner can keep that beast under control and only feed it what is necessary, then the owner has a tremendous advantage that affects both the cash flow and the profit and loss of the business. If the owner can control those two elements, then they can provide a better service, earn a better reputation, and demand a higher bed rate. Ultimately, they are running a business and not allowing the business to run them.

The Important Role Insurance Plays in Having Peace of Mind

Susan: What does it mean to owners if they do get the protection that they need?

Charley: Many aging baby boomers are finding the need to be placed into residential care while their adult children don't really know what to do with them. Currently, the state of California has a recognized bed count of between 165,000 to 175,000 beds. In 15 years, California has estimated a need for well over 925,000 beds to house all of these seniors and loved ones who are currently being dragged down by Alzheimer's, dementia or another crippling illness.

As I mentioned earlier, a lot of people get into this business to help others. They don't always know what they don't know and when it comes to insurance; this is very much the case. There is a lot of confusion in the field.

On the surface, insurance seems to be a commodity. The bigger Insurance companies constantly show advertisements telling us that. People tend to think, "Oh, insurance is all the same, if I can save a few dollars then I'm ahead of the curve." If their goal in having insurance is to just save as much money as possible, then stop reading because this book is not the right fit.

Having the right insurance coverage is as important for your business as receiving the right diagnosis from your personal Physician. You can start by talking with an insurance professional who is an expert in this field about specific needs like how your business runs, what are its greatest exposures and then tailoring policies to cover those specific areas. Putting the right coverage in place really allows the business owner to concentrate on running the business and providing excellent care, which is of paramount importance. If owners are tied up worrying about their insurance coverage, can they really focus on the day-to-day needs of the business and, more importantly, of the residents?

As an owner, you've spent your waking hours and countless sleepless nights thinking about "what if" questions that can be answered by an insurance professional. I would prefer owners to be in a worry-free place about the "what ifs", so they are able to use that energy to better serve their residents Having the correct insurance protects the business and shields the owner creating peace of mind.

The Right Insurance for Your RCFE

Susan: Tell us what owners need to know to get the right level of protection for their RCFE?

Charley: First, it's important to think about preserving the business and retaining all of the assets of the individual by meeting the legal requirements. On July 1st of 2015, the state of California passed Assembly Bill 1523, which required every residential care facility to have a $1 million / $3 million package for liability insurance. While 99.9% of the residential care facility owners know about this part, there are some parts that they don't know about, such as the legal requirement for care facility owners to have Workers Compensation insurance. Many times, I hear RCFE owners say, "I'm sub-contracting my employees from somebody else so I don't need that insurance," or, "My people are all 1099s." It is important to ensure that workers are classified correctly. Misclassification can result in significant liability. The IRS has provided guidelines to its agents to help determine worker status. In the past, a listing of 20 factors had been used in court decisions. In the back of this book you will find that listing. However, the actual determination is based on common law and recently IRS agents have been directed to focus on the overall situation rather than a strict interpretation of the 20 factors. The unique situation needs to take into consideration the relationship of the worker and the business. Worker determination depends primarily on the extent to which the employer exercises direction and control over the worker.

There was another Assembly Bill that passed on July 1, 2015. AB 2236 allows for increased punitive damages. If there is an injury or a death at an RCFE, the Department of Social Services can visit the place and say, "We are going to immediately assess you a $10,000 or $15,000 penalty." Many owners are unaware of that Bill.

Did you know that punitive damage coverage is available in most cases relatively inexpensively? It is a simple endorsement, but you need to know to ask. When I offer it, most of my clients take the extra coverage – it is a good value.

Susan: Wow. What other types of insurance do they need to know about?

Charley: Many RCFE facilities are located in converted tract or custom homes which, for the most part, were designed for a single family residence. At some point that house was insured with a Personal Lines policy – which was adequate when it was NOT occupied by a business.

When you are running a substantial business out of a home, as do all of the RCFEs, there must be a commercial policy on the house because personal lines policies from Farmers or Allstate or State Farm Insurance, etc. do not provide coverage for that business enterprise. If there is a loss during that period when a Personal Lines policy is in place, then it is most likely that the loss will not be covered by the Carrier. The claim will be denied.

They need a commercial grade policy. Did you know you can get coverage for business income if the structure has a covered loss that interrupts the cash flow of the business? That is only available in a commercial policy. It is a good coverage and a good value to keep the business running during a catastrophic event.

Another really important issue is that many RCFE owners will drive their residents to and from various appointments in their own personal vehicles. If they don't have the right kind of commercial auto endorsement on their car, there is zero coverage. Claims will not be paid. In many instances, people will tell me, "I have a policy with Farmers, State Farm, Geico, Allstate." From experience, I know that those policies specifically exclude this type of commercial driving because the resident is in your care, custody, and control. You are taking care of them for a fee; when you are moving them from place to place in a vehicle, the insurance world calls that 'livery'. It's like driving a taxi cab. In order to get proper coverage for that situation, you must have a commercial endorsement, called Hired and Non Owned Auto on your liability policy. If they were to shop this coverage as a single line item, the cost will be in the thousands of dollars. In most cases, we can attach this vital coverage to the policy for only a few hundred dollars and it covers not only the welfare of residents while they are being transported but also covers employees while they are driving between RCFE locations while on the job or running business errands in their own personal vehicle.

Many RCFE owners are unaware of this and they won't find out they are at risk until something happens and at that point it's too late.

After workman's compensation and liability, there are other types of insurance like EPLI (Employment Practice Liability Insurance). This type of insurance covers the owner if they fire somebody the wrong way, if they say something to an employee, or somebody else says something to an employee that is offensive while that employee is in their charge; they are held responsible for that.

Sometimes people will buy the cheapest insurance policy thinking they are saving money but in the end their policy includes a bunch of fluff coverage that doesn't really apply to their situation.

For instance, there is a coverage called First Dollar Defense which zeroes the deductible in the case of a liability claim. If you have a $1,000 deductible, it doesn't make sense to keep First Dollar Defense on the policy since the cost is often $300 dollars and up, it's not a good value and you don't need both. Since there are several other minor coverages similar to that one, you want to restructure your insurance coverage and add only the necessary endorsements that apply specifically to their situation.

This way the policy is tailored exactly to the owner's risk. A risk in Los Angeles certainly will have different needs than a risk in San Diego or San Francisco. One risk doesn't include driving the residents at all, so there is no need to get hired to non-owned auto coverage for that; however, hired and non-owned auto coverage may be necessary if the owner often sends their staff to run errands during business time, or maybe the staff travels between two or three different locations. Then, we definitely want to add the hired and non-owned auto coverage.

There is also the punitive damage coverage, which will pay for punitive fines that California assesses against a residential care facility. There is HIPPA insurance to protect privacy. We don't know exactly how the business runs unless we ask the right questions about these important details. If you get a policy from some clerk who is just keying your name into a system that spits out the cheapest price, that vanilla policy will most likely lack the coverage they need.

Susan: What steps can owners take to reduce their overall costs for insurance?

Charley: That's a great question and the answer is rather simple.

When the DSS comes out to inspect the RCFE, it needs to have zero citations and complaints. The underwriters who price the policies have access to a tremendous amount of information – they look at all the licensing web sites and dig into any complaints that are written up. If the RCFE has complaints that pertain to medications stored in an unlocked cabinet or food left out on a table – then the part of the Liability policy that will indemnify against that specific infraction may be priced higher, unless we can produce a viable explanation of why and how that infraction occurred. I have recently had underwriters who scour social media and referral / review sites in order to get a greater understanding of the public's attitude toward the facility. The best course is no citations then the underwriters has NO reason to trigger further and deeper investigation.

The RCFE Insurance Claims That Can Cause Higher Insurance Premiums

The good news is the actual claims ratio for RCFEs are very small, which speaks volumes for the people who run these businesses; they really take care of their residents. However, when a claim does go through, they tend to be very large. I recently had a case where a resident, who at times was combative; not to excess, but enough to be troublesome. This resident was being helped from a chair at the dining table to the sofa. During the transfer the resident was feisty enough to cause the caregiver to lose her grip. As the resident began to slip the caregiver had to grab the resident by the arm to arrest the fall. The arm grab created a bruise. Had the family and DSS been notified to inform them of the bruise then everything would have been alright. The issue was that the Owner of the RCFE was away for three days and the family had been to visit just after the bruise occurred – noting the Owner was not present, they assumed the worse, hired an Attorney and the claim was made then paid. For the next five years that insurance cost will not only be increased but it will be more difficult to secure coverage.

We had another issue where a caregiver who worked only part time at the RCFE put in a Workers Compensation claim for a Carpal Tunnel injury. Upon further investigation, we discovered that the injury was not sustained at the RCFE but at the Retail store the caregiver worked as their other part time job. A job whose duties involved scanning checkout items and pricing shelf goods over and over, all day long. I need to qualify this one: the client came to me for help because their original agent had ignored their requests. I did not originate this policy, and that is where the problem began. The Work Comp carrier didn't fight or investigate the claim. They just took the loss and wrote the check. That payment, although covered 100% by the Workers Compensation policy, eventually put my friend out of business. Why? Because at his renewal of the State Mandated Work Comp policy, due to the severity of the loss, his ratios of premium paid vs claims paid created an increase of over 300% in his Workers Compensation insurance. His cost of doing business, quite simply ballooned to such a volume that looking forward it would be impossible to generate a profit, or even a break even. He was forced to close his doors.

Susan: Are there some mistakes that you often see RCFE owners make?

Charley: Certainly, the most common mistake I see is when owners shop price and price alone. It is very common to have two almost identical policies – each showing the limits necessary to comply with State Laws with 30% or even 40% difference in cost. Many owners that I meet with are amazed and even angry when I point out to them, after reading their policy, that the exclusions in their current policy have reduced their coverage to an almost worthless amount of protection. I get it that we are all running businesses and we need to control costs. However, I strongly suggest that owners sit down with and discuss the endorsements and exclusions in their policy with a Licensed Insurance Professional who specializes in commercial insurance for RCFEs. It really all boils down to tailoring the insurance policy for your specific needs and coverage. A professional agent knows this and should offer to make the time to put the protection in place to safe guard the business they have worked so hard to create.

How to Get the Insurance Protection You Need for Your RCFE

Susan: How can someone find out if they have the right insurance protection for their RCFE?

Charley: This is my area of expertise. I know the industry trends and the traps that can cripple an RCFE operation. I know the actual insurance companies, the carriers who are in business for the long haul, as well as those who may not be charging enough to stay in business; and that's a very scary proposition. When a business owner buys an insurance policy that is so much less expensive than every other policy in the marketplace, that should be a red flag. The company will stick around for a little while, but they will probably have to leave fairly quickly, because they will not have enough money to pay claims. We see it often. We call it cash flow underwriting. It's when a carrier is buying market share, through a lower cost offering and not properly investing those premiums back into the company because claims costs will eventually make that carrier unprofitable and thereby creating a shell that eventually collapses.

What's at risk if you are not properly insured? Basically, everything that you own is at risk (material assets like your home and cars, plus 25% of all future earnings for the next 10 years), with the exception of an ERISA (Employee Retirement

Income Security Act) protected retirement Insurance is activated when a tragedy occurs. You need a policy that takes care of the big stuff that will cripple a family for a generation. But you get what you pay for. Writing a check for the premium is not fun, but in my experience, my clients are happy when they call me and ask if they have coverage and I tell them: "Don't worry, we've got that covered." Insurance is a transfer risk. You pay some money to have the carrier take the big hits. That's how it's designed. Your Professional Insurance Agent should be part of your management team.

I like to take a quick insurance audit when I meet with new clients. I review their prior coverage; it takes me about 15 minutes to do an insurance audit because I'm familiar with all of the policies. Usually I know that in X Company, their policy has "Y" kind of language and I need to look out for these "Z" traps. For instance, one company may give the Cadillac experience, but there is one little endorsement that needs to be added to make it the super Cadillac. It's complicated because the language is unfamiliar to most of us.

After a quick review of the prior policies, I like to gather some specific information about the business and operations. This really helps me zero in on the needs of that RCFE. I then ask for a copy of the facility license, its latest inspection, and any plan of corrective action in rebuttal to that inspection. Now, I can move forward with the insurance quote. I may also need to have something called a 'loss run', or a scorecard of their insurance experiences with current and past carriers. This record states something like this:

"The business has been with us for two to five years and they have not had any losses," or, "This business has had insurance with us during this same period of time; they have had these losses, this is how much was paid out, and this is how much is in reserve."

Charley: My job as a professional insurance agent is to listen to how your business runs, and then apply your insurance dollars in places where they will do the most good for you and offer the most value. My phone number is 805-379-2022. My email address is: charley@bealsagency.com. Email is a great way to catch me because I check it all the time. I would love to sit down with you and take a look at where you may be exposed to more risk than you know about.

Susan: Thank you, Charley. As you said, if you got into this business from the caretaking side, I can see how a lot of these business issues can get overlooked because they seem really scary. Thank you for simplifying the big words for us, because I think this is obviously mission critical, especially for RCFE owners. I think it is fabulous that you offer to do an insurance audit for them.

Charley: Thank you. I'm trying to bring a little sanity to this craziness that is the insurance world in the State of California. I really want to help people get a better understanding of it, which will lead to a better insurance experience. That way, they can actually focus on what's really important, taking care of the residents who have had full lives and are now in the sunset of their lives.

Here's How to Get the Insurance Protection You Need for Your California RCFE

You already know running a home care facility takes round the clock care and attention. You also know that there are certain liabilities that come from running an RCFE, such as a resident getting hurt, or an employee having an accident. The confusing part is knowing how make sure you have the right insurance so your livelihood is not in jeopardy when you have a large or small accident at your facility.

That's where we come in. We help people just like you ensure you have the right insurance coverage so you can focus on what you do best, which is giving the highest level of care you can for the residents.

Step 1: Call us for a quick insurance audit. We'll review your coverage to make sure you have the right insurance coverage for your facility.

Step 2: If necessary, we will then source for you the best insurance that makes sense for your business and show you where you are exposed to unnecessary risk.

Step 3: We take it from here and continue to monitor your insurance needs. If something changes, we can help you incorporate the changes so you are still adequately covered.

Most people think they are saving money when they get a lower quote for insurance. Not all policies are equal though and you don't want to be the guy who did not have enough or the right kind of insurance.

Now you can get the insurance protection you need and sleep well at night knowing you are covered.

If you'd like us to help, just send an email to: Charley@BealsAgency.com or call us at 805-379-2022 and we will take it from there.

The 20 factors identified by the IRS are as follows:

1. **Instructions:** If the person for whom the services are performed has the right to require compliance with instructions, this indicates employee status.

2. **Training:** Worker training (e.g., by requiring attendance at training sessions) indicates that the person for whom services are performed wants the services performed in a particular manner (which indicates employee status).

3. **Integration:** Integration of the worker's services into the business operations of the person for whom services are performed is an indication of employee status.

4. **Services rendered personally:** If the services are required to be performed personally, this is an indication that the person for whom services are performed is interested in the methods used to accomplish the work (which indicates employee status).

5. **Hiring, supervision, and paying assistants:** If the person for whom services are performed hires, supervises or pays assistants, this generally indicates employee status. However, if the worker hires and supervises others under a contract pursuant to which the worker agrees to provide material and labor and is only responsible for the result, this indicates independent contractor status.

6. **Continuing relationship:** A continuing relationship between the worker and the person for whom the services are performed indicates employee status.

7. **Set hours of work:** The establishment of set hours for the worker indicates employee status.

8. **Full time required:** If the worker must devote substantially full time to the business of the person for whom services are performed, this indicates employee status. An independent contractor is free to work when and for whom he or she chooses.

9. **Doing work on employer's premises:** If the work is performed on the premises of the person for whom the services are performed, this indicates employee status, especially if the work could be done elsewhere.

10. **Order or sequence test:** If a worker must perform services in the order or sequence set by the person for whom services are performed, that shows the worker is not free to follow his or her own pattern of work, and indicates employee status.

11. **Oral or written reports:** A requirement that the worker submit regular reports indicates employee status.

12. **Payment by the hour, week, or month:** Payment by the hour, week, or month generally points to employment status; payment by the job or a commission indicates independent contractor status.

13. **Payment of business and/or traveling expenses.** If the person for whom the services are performed pays expenses, this indicates employee status. An employer, to control expenses, generally retains the right to direct the worker.

14. **Furnishing tools and materials:** The provision of significant tools and materials to the worker indicates employee status.

15. **Significant investment:** Investment in facilities used by the worker indicates independent contractor status.

16. **Realization of profit or loss:** A worker who can realize a profit or suffer a loss as a result of the services (in addition to profit or loss ordinarily realized by employees) is generally an independent contractor.

17. **Working for more than one firm at a time:** If a worker performs more than de Minim is services for multiple firms at the same time, that generally indicates independent contractor status

18. **Making service available to the general public:** If a worker makes his or her services available to the public on a regular and consistent basis, that indicates independent contractor status.

19. **Right to discharge:** The right to discharge a worker is a factor indicating that the worker is an employee.

20. **Right to terminate:** If a worker has the right to terminate the relationship with the person for whom services are performed at any time he or she wishes without incurring liability, that indicates employee status.

More recently, the IRS has identified three categories of evidence that may be relevant in determining whether the requisite control exists under the common-law test and has grouped illustrative factors under these three categories: (1) behavioral control; (2) financial control; and (3) relationship of the parties.

The IRS emphasizes that factors in addition to the 20 factors identified in 1987 may be relevant, that the weight of the factors may vary based on the circumstances, that relevant factors may change over time, and that all facts must be examined.

Generally, individuals who follow an independent trade, business, or profession in which they offer services to the public are not employees. Courts have recognized that a highly educated or skilled worker does not require close supervision; therefore, the degree of day-to-day control over the worker's performance of services is not particularly helpful in determining the worker's status. Courts have considered other factors in these cases, tending to focus on the individual's ability to realize a profit or suffer a loss as evidenced by business investments and expenses.

https://www.irs.gov/pub/irs-utl/x-26-07.pdf